I0450575

GLOBAL ANARCHY

State, Society and International Politics

Zulfiqar Shah

Createspace, An Amazon Compan

DEDICATED TO THE WORLD CITIZENS

CONTENTS

ZULFIQAR SHAH

ACKNOWLEDGMENTS

The author has edited and compiled the essays and articles
published Daily Kathmandu Post, Nepal, Daily Afghanistan Times,
Kabul, and the websites of Russia Direct, Moscow as well as Russian
Council in International Affairs, Moscow

DANGEROUS MEANS

World politics since World War II has one highly common manifestation. The world powers since last century have turned conflicts into wars and transformed wars into proxy violence in bids to attain their legitimate or illegitimate interests. If the cold war strategies, the post-Cold War interests games, the post-9/11 situation and the recent Islamic State (ISIS) phenomena are reviewed deeply, it becomes crystal clear that the various powers have almost re-phrased the same old strategic modus operandi in the respective regions of the world.

Whenever individuals, political groups, regions, and world power blocs are involved in harsh competitions, they use legitimate and illegitimate means including conflicts to win certain geo-strategic regions and fight their interests. It is observed hitherto that the warring, conflicting, or competing powers neither care about minimum fundamental political morality nor do they formulate strategies to minimize destructive after effects.

Religion in Cold War

If we take example of the Cold War, the capitalist bloc had chosen religion as a means to counter and defeat the rise and influence of communism. Cold War is over now but the Islamic extremism yet did not come to a full stop. It seems that at the level of strategic planning, the powers do not think deeper about the means and tools of conflicts in a manner that their modus operandi stop causing further damage once whatsoever goals are achieved. This has caused great damage to harmony and human security in the world.

There is a common inclination in the international politics to make scapegoats of others for one's own blunders. It is an open secret that in the Cold War North America, Western and Scandinavian Europe, Australia, the Kingdom of Saudi Arabia, Pakistan, and some other countries from Asia and Africa were part of the 'capitalist bloc' led by the USA against the 'communist bloc' led by the USSR, which is now replaced mainly by Russia. Almost all countries in the capitalist bloc used, supported, and facilitated all means to defeat the USSR. One of those means was creating Islamist fighters against communism. When China came into conflict with the USSR over some territorial issues, it also started supporting the capitalist bloc and the Mujahedeen through Pakistan during the late 1970s and 1980s. Surprisingly, the same fraternity now criticizes the USA alone for creating Mujahedeen, while the rest of the partners are being forgiven. If the use of religion in a very retrogressive way for the politics of interests has proved devastative, all of those who supported this means are responsible for that. Hence, they are also commonly responsible for solving the problems that arose as a consequence. Criticizing only one country would be unjust.

Long term damage

States necessarily bring along war, and conflicts and competitions of interests are by products of state institutions. But this does not mean that to achieve their interests the world community may become irresponsible enough to use means that are highly destructive for humanity. The use of Islamic extremism for specific interests has already devastated humanity as well as numerous societies around the globe and now poses a huge challenge to overall international security. No doubt the world is paying for its own deeds in the form of security challenges and their economic consequences. Had the world not decided on choosing to extremise Islam in 1970s, it would not have been reaping Islamist destruction today. The outcomes of the Cold War use of Islamic extremism have proved that as long as the world community does not respect fundamental humanistic principles in choosing their means, tools and techniques in their competition of interests, in the long run they lose more than what they immediately gain. Planning in a bid to pursue interests needs to seek a comprehensive strategy that makes sure humanity is not going to suffer in the long term. Therefore the means and tools of interest achievement need to have no or few side effects and no long term destructive aspects. This is a prerequisite for world powers to also adopt better strategic exit plans once their interests are achieved. The world community needs to adopt as a fundamental principal to pursue their interest in any geographical region in a manner that the legitimate interests and rights of that regions' indigenous population may not be damaged. This can be seen as a contemporary interpretation of the Vedic term 'coexistence'.

Published in Daily The Kathmandu Post on November 30, 2014

A CULTURE OF STATE

Is it because of a diversity of interests, thoughts and wisdom that the world today is becoming such a knotty patchwork? Yes, it is an issue of disorientation in decision-making at the state, society and world levels.

The developments and phenomenal failures of our era talk volumes. The turning of the Arab Spring into a summer of discontent; the endless journey to disillusionment in Afghanistan; the mercenary-syndicalism and their popping up in Iraq after Syria as ISIS; and the deepening global insecurity that now faces Ukraine and the Korean peninsula are indicators of nothing but an ailing state apparatus and failing policy practices among the 'almighty establishments' countrywide as well as at the regional and global levels. If there be an end of the history, it will never come along Francis Fukuyama's line of conflicting civilizations; rather, it may emerge out of the debris of world states, which are only a source of global anarchy. We can say to a certain extent and in definite terms, that anarcho-syndicalism of its own kind among some states has become the ugliest characteristic of contemporary statehood.

Voluntarily fragmented

The state is an institution which makes legitimate use of violence to maintain peace, security and the socio-economic order. But it has not only been violating its foundational roots, but also dispossessing this very fundamental characteristic of the 'legitimate use of violence', albeit in different forms in developed, developing and under-developed countries. This has different manifestations in federations, countries and geo-political and strategic regions around the world.

The US, France and the UK are classical models in the developed world for this kind of voluntary dispossession. The separation of war-making and security institutions in the form of privatized light and heavy arms industry, private detectors and intelligence firms and officiated mercenaries is what apparently provides a fancy outlook to what otherwise may be called the unethical acts of a para-state organism. Political ethics come under question when weapon manufacturing as well as snooping into people's lives is outsourced to industrial and professional groups.

In developing countries like Pakistan, for example, the state has voluntarily shared its violence-making capacity with terrorist outfits. These are the jihadists, Talibans, urban terrorists and mafias. They are state-sponsored militant wings of political parties that were either born out of the Pakistani establishment or partnered with it later on. They are viral and infiltrative. Borders do not exist for these elements as they roam easily around the continent and the world. Internally, they keep society harassed, tamed and fragmented, and have been strategically enabled to counter freedom movements in Sindh and Balochistan. They also help prolong the military establishment's rule in Pakistan.

Some African countries, among under-developed nations, are the worst examples of this situation, where everything exists but the state. The Tutsi-Hutu case in Rwanda is an example of a situation where the state collapsed as a contender for the legitimate use of violence. The state was the warring tribes, tribal militia and warlords. It did not want to voluntarily withdraw its capacity for violence making in favor of a fragile state.

These three phenomena have different impacts, manifestations and outcomes. The common element in all of them is their inter-connectedness. This may be called the upside-down order, the epicentering of endless conflicts, thereby, posing potential challenges to international security. One might legitimately find a cliental relationship between the three. The worst scenario of all, however, is the case of countries like Pakistan. This has proved to be a challenging security risk not only for the citizenry and the federated provinces, but also for neighboring countries and the regions, as well as the developed world. It seems as though there is no end to colonialism, be it internal or external, physical or virtual.

Non-globalism

There is only one order in the world today—disorder. Structurally, this disorder is gradually embedding itself into regional and national interests, hardly giving any space to the very notion of the political world or the global village. Globalization today is very much paradoxical, as it is the globalization of backward and developing countries in the interests of the rest. The naïve example of this is the patent rights of 'commodities', in which the very concept of globalization is betrayed by seeking patent rights to natural produce, which, by all means , are the collective property of human kind. Can a grain, fruit, tree, herb and shrub be patented?

Today, international security is also more fragile than in the past. Swiftly changing regional games in Eurasia, Central Asia, the Middle East and the Korean peninsula indicate the possibility of a multilateral war, if not a third world war. Engagement in Afghanistan needs to be reconsolidated conclusively, which requires a collectively agreed upon exceptionalism by the engaging powers. The re-emergence of issues like the Iraq crisis, attempts to reclaim its bygone power by Russia, China's assertion in the Pacific Ocean and the UK's snub to the European Union are the results of ambiguous and non-representative national interests as well as the absence of collectively agreed exceptionalism among world powers.

This is a very crucial time. The world has to sit together to address these issues collectively. At least, the US, UK, France, Russia, China, Germany, India and Japan have to develop a consensus on their foreign policy exceptionalism concerning Afghanistan, the Israel-Palestine conflict, re-creation of a Kurdish republic out of Iraq, settling the Iraq issue and addressing the issues of Sindh and Balochistan.

Reforming statehood

In fact, the reboot and upgrade in the state apparatus, practicing collective foreign policy excptionalism, conflict resolution, appropriate globalization, mannered international trade and justifiable national interests are interdependent. Hence, they contribute to the global order, stability and international security.

The moment has arrived for the world community to analyze and help foster an exclusive shift in the state apparatuses around the world. Concrete steps are required to re-define the role of a state in its legitimacy over violence and the assurance of minimum civil conditions for peace and economic well being. Simultaneously, the time has come for states to derestrict the agenda of 'national interest', which hitherto has been confined to the establishments of countries. Until approved by the citizenry, the 'national-interest' can appropriately be termed 'state-interest' as often; it does not include the citizens' will. This alone can lead us to a peaceful world, true globalization and a global order for stability, peace and international security.

Published in Daily The Kathmandu Post on August 31, 2014

FORBIDDEN QUESTIONS

Humans have forgotten so many things. They have forgotten to ask fundamental questions to reach at priori and a priori realities. Sometimes these questions are forbidden, but mostly they find no way for expression because together, we have virtually banned logical thinking. These questions number in the millions but we can only highlight a few.

Reality of religions
Pulpits across the globe are dominated by the essence of religion. This is the point where religious stereotypes have cast out the logic of theology, and the torch bearers of theology have resisted theosophy. Although the major task and niche of our times is to reconnect theosophy and philosophy, we have downgraded our religious understanding to the bottom.

What we have forgotten is to make religions contemporary. Just imagine if Hinduism, Buddhism, Judaism, Christianity, and Islam were practically translated, interpreted, and adopted into the realities of our own times. For example, the Vedic interpretation of Aryans and non-Aryans were ones who were civilized and ones who were not. But the existing definition of Aryanism is restricted to certain practices, traditions, and ethnic origins. So if the Vedic interpretation of Aryanism is adopted contemporarily, we will see that all those who are part of a collective human society that professes religious tolerance, ethnic and cultural diversity, justice, and humanism are the true Aryans.

Vedas are the first scripted holy books of human wisdom. The Rig Veda, the first such treatise, was said to be written in Shivasthan in Sindh, the city now known as Sewhan—one of the centers of Sufism in South Asia. All religions owe something to the Vedas. But we have forgotten to adopt and honor them. Since they are the collective property of humanity, they need to be re-explored, re-defined, and re-incorporated into our contemporary times.

Moreover, Arabs and Muslims have a fundamental responsibility to Hinduism, Buddhism, Jainism, Judaism, and Christianity. One of the verses in the holy Quran mentions that the Momins (faithful) are those who believe equally in all holy books and all of the prophets sent by the God. This means that Muslims generally and Arabs particularly have to respect all religions. Arabs, especially, have a cultural responsibility to Judaism and Christianity.

In the same vein, can a state have religion? Not at all. A state has only one religion—statism.

Israel-Palestine question

Most of us mix the contemporary conflict in Israel-Palestine with the historical justification of Israel. When Israel was re-created after thousands years, and Jews finally returned to their historical homeland, the Al-Azhar University of Egypt was the first Muslim institution to gave a religious verdict in favor of Israel.

No doubt, one cannot snatch the right of a nation to return to their homeland. There are some other aspects of this issue as well, which most Muslims are unaware of. When Israel was formed, the Israeli leadership gave Palestinians two options—either a separate Palestinian state or to collectively live in Israel-Palestine. Palestinians in the early 1950s did not choose either and some Arab and non-Arab countries advised the Palestinians to fight. Today, they are fighting for the same option that they discarded six decades ago. Who is responsible for this? The Palestinian leadership and their Arab instigators! This historical reality is one important lesson of history.

Failure of communism

Marx never said that the abolition of private property means the handing over of your resources to the state. He said that all powers and decisions should be transferred to the communes of people. He was talking about a transfer of power to the people, a highly articulated and enhanced role of the people in the governance of their own. That was the reason he once said that the fundamental task of communism is to create a new human. Almost all of the calmingly socialist and communist revolutions pursued this goal in opposite manners. They simply handed over responsibilities to the state and not the communes. Thus, the practical manifestations of socialist states were non-Marxist. Ultimately, human society has to go in that direction, but through an evolutionary and transformative process.

Mistaken identities

Most of the terminologies within English journalism are coined by media houses in the US, the UK and Europe. Some of these terminologies are discriminatory. Can there be any 'Islamic or Buddhist terrorism'? No religion professes terrorism. Can there be 'Muslim terrorism'? Impossible. But these inappropriate terms dominate the discourse and narrative of our times. Reality is entirely different. Almost all, except for a few, terror groups proclaim Salafism as their school of thought. Salafis are less than one percent of the Muslim population of the world and lesser than two percent of the Sunni sect of Islam. Therefore, even terms like 'Sunni Terrorism' are discriminatory.

What we have forgotten as humans is to find unity among diversity—of religions, cultures, thoughts, disciplines of education, and intellectual discourses. We have unconsciously or forcibly forbidden none other than ourselves from thinking outside the box and reflecting literally or logically. And, therefore we have lost harmony and world peace. Humanism will only come through welcoming diversity and dissent and seeking unity among diversified realities.

Published in Daily The Kathmandu Post on December 28, 2014

A FULL STOP TO THE 20TH CENTURY

It was neither the end nor the beginning. It was just a calendar-adjustment globally to the tune of the 21st century. Nevertheless, the inception of the new century some fifteen years ago ought to have left a deep socio-psychological impression on everyone. The global citizenry yearning for change wanted socio-political and eco-economic transformations in the real-time history of their own living generation. Have we really inched ahead, and tried to unbutton the change waiting to be? Not yet! Then, rest assured that the time has come to dig at the microcosm of a time-bound demand for this unavoidable discourse.

Polarized diversity

We are undergoing a troika of issues and happenings—the transition from a unipolar to a multipolar world; the increasing globalization of the state and the corporate sector in comparison with society and the resulting widening gap between state and society as well as global frictions; and the menace of terrorism that uses religion as a tool to create brainwashed homicidals.

Our travel from the post-Soviet collapse to re-engagement in Afghanistan followed by Russia's annexation of Crimea—no matter legitimately or otherwise—is nothing but a reflection of the emerging multiple centers of global power. What varying degree of geopolitical and strategic spread they possess is of little concern. Hence, an entirely new course of political and academic discourse is needed around this faster-than-ferries development.

Stagnation in change

The maverick aspect of time and space in the contemporary socio-political and economic course has been the unending conflict between the statuesque and change. This phenomenon is visible everywhere, with a variation in degrees.

The unity and later on constructive differences on the issue of Afghanistan; the gradual emergence of India among the Asian powers; the Arab Spring and social movements around the world; the liberation of Kosovo and South Sudan; and the annexation of Crimea are the threadbares of political developments, which need wisdom for appropriate disposition. A wisdom that is beyond the scope of Machiavelli and Clausewitz.

Moreover, the threat of new conflicts among the gradually multi-polarizing world that blinks now in Eurasia and then in Syria has made us all prone to a feeling of anxiety concerning global insecurity. As if all powers want to do everything for their interests alone, forgetting that the world requires a strategic balance and the fulfillment of the interests of larger global stakeholders. The world, however, cannot avoid mutually, bilaterally and collectively-agreed upon exceptionalism in their foreign policies for completing the unfinished tasks of the bygone century.

State-society honeymoon
The emergence of new social movements, fostering of freedom movements and secessionism, an increase in the role of the international community, particularly the United Nations, and the resurgence of conflicts in almost all major continents are indicative of a rethink about the relations between today's society and the state.

The world has never seen a honeymoon between the state and society since both were yet to become full-fledged adults. However, the state has matured earlier than society, particularly in the developing world and the global south. Therefore, a new academic and analytical discourse is needed to engage with so that this new century may prove to be an appropriate time for state-society partnership for human development and collective achievements for attaining a sustainable future for our generations. It does not only require a transformation between state-society relationships. It also requires a new social contract between both so that ongoing socio-political movements may culminate into fruitful ends to the better interests of all.

Besides, the world has to give a final verdict for old and new regional movements brewing around hotspots like Kurdistan, Tamil, Sindh and Balochistan.

Out of the box
Central and South Asia, as well as Africa, are the potential economic zones for the coming decades, which we need to focus on. Therefore a

grand worldly, if not universal, cross can understandably be forecasted predeceasing the future shift in the policies of the United States, Canada, the United Kingdom, France, Russia, China, India, Germany, Japan, Brazil, Australia, South Africa and South Korea. None in the future will be able to bypass this niche of old and new powers in the corridors of global maneuvering. If seen in this new developing arena, any irritant, like a possible Russia, European Union and US conflict, may stall mature engagements, like Afghanistan. If this is seen in the perspective of an alarmingly changing climate and its impacts on economies, a deep maturity towards the wider range of issues becomes inevitable.

The remaining half of the ongoing and the whole of the next decade need visionary, calculated, and long lasting decisions from the world leadership. The challenges are enormous—eliminating the chances of large-scale wars; culminating the Afghanistan engagement into a meaningful end; strengthening the West's relationships with Iran and India to further the Asian partnership; deciding about new nations yearning to become sovereign states; reforming the UN; redefining globally agreed legal instruments of sovereignty; creating a forum within the UN for the federated states of federations where they may exercise rights to self-determination without waging wars; and mapping global realignment along collective interests. Actions like these are required for a real transformation from the 20th century into the 21st.

Published in Daily The Kathmandu Post on June 1, 2014

II
CONTEMPORARY ISSUES

ENDGAME AFGHANISTAN

The largest and most diverse military movement in the globe after World War II will come to an end this year in Afghanistan. Unlike the messy world wars of the last century, the conclusion of this mini world war against proxy war-making groups promises neither sustained stability in South Central Asia nor offers a by-product similar to the League of Nations that emerged after World War I. Amid the well-received news in Afghanistan regarding the quitting of international forces, Afghans and neighboring countries are still uncertain about the Afghan endgame.

Strategic centre
Why is Afghanistan so important that attempts have been made to capture it for the last couple of centuries? It seems that the world has reached the conclusion that whoever rules Afghanistan will rule the world. In 2012, a Chinese company outbid a Russian company for the biggest copper reservoirs in the world in the Lugar province of Afghanistan. Consequently, a friendly race between the Shanghai Cooperation Organisation (SCO) and the Collective Security Treaty Organisation (CSTO) of the former Soviet Union states began. Similarly, the conflict between Pakistan and India has been the central point of the Afghan drama in which Pakistan used the 'strategic tool' of the Taliban in an attempt to undertake a major neighboring role in the post-International Security Assistance Force (ISAF) scene.

Meanwhile, Iran has kept its unnamed relations with the US in the Afghan context using its Persian demographic presence. China and the US have never been on the same page whenever the issue of the Red Army's engagement arises; however, the Chinese have never stepped back while economic engagements as well as benefits are still central. Many players like Turkey, Germany, the United Arab Emirates and Saudi Arabia have been yearning for their roles too, no matter how low profile they may be. The contest over neighborly engagement claims are between Pakistan, Iran and Tajikistan. The three, besides sharing borders, also share an ethno-linguistic demography with Afghanistan.

Global failure

The failure in the costliest war of our times is mainly due to competing interests amid strategies that are alien to the ground realities of warfare as well as state building. All the major stakeholders have their own interests, issues and limits in Afghanistan. Pakistan has been at the core of Afghanistan's war troubles. Its notion to install a Pakistan-friendly Pashtun government in Kabul created a battlefield of an entirely different nature in the broader strategic arena of the war game. The Taliban were a major factor behind the destabilizing war in Afghanistan and consequently invited counter proxy wars from the other side. Besides, Pakistan has played a minimal role in the reconstruction of Afghanistan. On the other hand, India has used its soft power in Afghanistan by avoiding a military presence like China and Iran. Besides, it has played a vital role in infrastructure development, strengthening of democratic institutions and human resources enhancement.

Furthermore, the Taliban phenomenon is deeply rooted in the matrix of the India-Afghanistan foreign policy of Pakistan. Statecraft in Pakistan is dominated by an ethnic Punjabi majority; and the invasion of Afghanistan was an old Punjabi dream of Raja Ranjit Singh (1780-1839) who captured Peshawar from Afghanistan in 1818. Peshawar is now capital of the Pakistani province of Khyber Pakhtunkhuwa. Contemporary Pakistan's Afghan policy is based on the issue of the Durand Line which it wants Afghanistan to officially recognize as an international border. Besides, Pakistan wants a Pashtun-dominated government in Kabul to minimize the Indian, Iranian, Tajik, Russian and US roles there, especially the Northern Alliance. Pakistan has attempted to regain its centrality regarding Afghanistan; however, India has attained strategic superiority by establishing its first foreign airbase in Farkhor, Tajikistan and supporting electricity transfer to Afghanistan and road construction to Post Abbas in Iran.

China's internal security interests in Afghanistan are peace and political stability. While maintaining a low profile, China has professed support for an "Afghan-led and owned peace process" and reconciliation for sustainable sovereignty. China has also rendered infrastructure support. Meanwhile, Russia has been tactically supporting the ISAF by opening its territory for non-lethal supply to NATO, sharing intelligence and providing financial support. Russia, along with the Central Asian States (CAS), considers Afghanistan directly proportionate to their internal security regarding narcotics smuggling as well as the infiltration of Islamist terrorists. Besides, the landlocked CAS can only access the warm waters of the Persian Gulf via Afghanistan from either Port Abbas in Iran or Karachi and Guwadar in Pakistan.

The US position is the most important which envisions an economically integrated Central South Asian region where Afghanistan plays a central role. This is the point where engagement with or without the Taliban is the only option. On the southern borders of Afghanistan, Iran has remained on the edges. The Taliban, who follow the Salafi school of Saudian Islam, does not ideologically suit Iran. Besides, Iran's traditional Arab rivals have supported them. There are still possibilities of Iran's cooperation with the US in Afghanistan; however, Iran has serious security concerns over US military bases in Kandahar and Mazar-e-Sharif.

Possibilities

The international community has always underestimated the Afghani capacity for governance, and international forces have either been reluctant or extraordinarily slow in their capacity building and transferring of authority before 2014. Meanwhile, transparent, free and fair elections in Afghanistan are another issue of contention. Besides, the ethnic composition of the state apparatus in Afghanistan has not been inclusive. Today, the structural and institutional framework and the development of Afghan national governance is a matter of high importance along with transparency in governance. Besides, local governance would be the only way for the Afghan people to defend themselves from instability and rogue elements.

The most important issue is the federal structure of Afghanistan. Until a highly inclusive federal structure with proportionate inclusion of ethnic groups is made possible, there will be no full stop to civil wars. The UN along with other stakeholders should play a vital role in this regard. Afghanistan is still on a razor edge with various possible scenarios of post-ISAF sustenance including a Taliban partnership, Taliban takeover of Kabul or the shirked rite of Kabul over the country. Three factors are highly important. They are global support for the Afghan government in comparison with the Taliban, the role of a secular Afghan majority in the state field, and logically debasing the Taliban's anti-foreign sentiments after the ISAF's withdrawal.

Published in Daily The Kathmandu Post on July 28, 2013

WHY CRIMEA WILL RESONATE BEYOND EUROPE

Crimea's recent referendum on joining Russia has opened up a broader debate about sovereignty, political legitimacy and realpolitik in the modern world.

Until now, the debate over Crimea has primarily manifested itself as a scholarly discourse about the secession rights of individual states, especially within federations that are experiencing intra-state conflicts. This means, however, that what happens in Crimea also has implications for other secessionist movements around the world.

The debate over Crimea also has crucial implications for any discussion of realpolitik within the realm of international relations. This aspect of the debate goes well beyond any academic and political discourses about legitimacy and sovereignty, focusing instead on global priorities and national, regional, and continental interests.

In short, the situation in Ukraine has kicked off a broader debate about a realignment in a new multi-polar world, where competition between various global powers could be transformed as a result of how they respond to new conflicts of interest.

Crimea's impact around the world

The triangle of conflicting interests at this stage is between Russia, the United States and the European Union. However, the situation in Crimea could ultimately create a window for reviewing the role of the North Atlantic Treaty Organization (NATO), the emerging role of China and India in global politics and a dramatic paradigm shift for the Afghanistan endgame, where global stakes appear to be reaching their climax.

If this situation in Crimea is not addressed appropriately, it will ultimately have some adverse impacts on the highly volatile geostrategic affairs in South Asia, Central Asia, the Middle East, and the Asia-Pacific region.

It could also increase the historical distance between Eastern European Slav nations and West European Anglo-Saxon nations, and to a certain extent, between Eastern European and Scandinavian nations.

Precedents for Crimea in international law

Primarily, the secession of Crimea from Ukraine and its annexation to the Russian Federation falls within the purview of the right of self-determination. However, it also falls within the jurisdiction of several United Nations General Assembly (UNGA) and United Nations Security Council (UNSC) resolutions as well as international legal instruments, arrangements and precedence concerning the secession of Bangladesh (1971), East Timor (2002), Kosovo (2008) and South Sudan (2011).

Thus, it would be unsound to reason that the will demonstrated by the people of Crimea as well as the parliament of the Crimea is against international law, particularly when Crimea had special arrangements with Ukraine, according to which Crimea had its own parliament and constitution within Ukraine.

It becomes a further irony that Ukraine, which seceded from the former Soviet Union through almost similar instruments, is denouncing the same measures when they are adopted by Crimea.

Redefining sovereignty

Around the world, questions related to the 'sovereignty' of member states of the United Nations have become a major element of the debate regarding Crimea.

Academically speaking, the term 'sovereignty' is not always as easy to define as it might seem. The discussion and use of the term "sovereignty" in this case, as we saw in earlier cases, can distort the debate. It is, quite simply, a simultaneously difficult and ambiguous concept to define.

Sovereignty is not - and can never be - absolute. In so many ways, it is a relative concept and reality. For example, the concept of sovereignty in federations around the world has an entirely different connotation than for individual nations and states. The sovereignty of Japan, for example, is highly different from the sovereignty of Pakistan.

In a federation, sovereignty fundamentally is rooted within the federating states, which voluntarily (or, in some cases, involuntarily) is given to the Federation through the instruments, agreements and arrangements of joining the Federation. Sovereignty, either directly or indirectly, remains a principal part of the constitutions of Federations.

Sovereignty forms the basis (both in concept and principle) for thinking about military institutions in a federation, where federating states can create their own military regiments. It also determines the domains of coastal and international water rights between Federations and the Federating States.

And, in some cases, it defines issues related to borders, ports and use of air space. Therefore, the secession of Crimea might be legitimized in accordance with international law, geopolitical precedence and the political principles, philosophy and practices relating to sovereignty, especially within federations.

Lessons learned from Crimea

The Ukraine crisis has increased the chances of destabilizing the peace and security environment around the globe. It also threatens to turn the current geopolitical order upside down, or at least, result in new conflicts of interests between global players.

The situation potentially will not only put the Afghanistan issue at high risk, but also may give leverage to the elements of destabilization around the world, whether in Asia or the Middle East, to take advantage of the new emerging situation. Besides, it also involves a new need for both the European Union and the Eurasia Economic Union to revisit their policies and strategic priorities.

It is essential that the U.S., EU and Russia sit together at a round table and resolve this issue appropriately before it gives new impetus to disruption and conflict elsewhere. They will need to consider how the U.S. and Russia can reach a compromise, how Russia can assure the rest of the world that it will not intrude into other Eastern European countries, and what should be the role of India and China in resolving similar types of conflict around the globe.

After all, any false step at this stage can open up a new Pandora's Box of militarization and armed conflicts around the globe.

Published in Russia Direct, Moscow on March 24, 2014

AFGHAN ENDGAME: IS A STABLE AFGHANISTAN POSSIBLE?

With International Security Assistance Forces (ISAF) slated to withdraw from Afghanistan in 2014, how will U.S. and Russian security interests in the region align?

The history of global intervention in Afghanistan over the past two centuries has been one of colossal failure. However, it's still too early to tell whether the presence of international forces there during the last decade, as well as the recent plan to withdraw these forces by 2014, will ultimately be judged as a success or failure.

After previous unsuccessful interventions by Britain and Russia during the nineteenth and twentieth centuries, the contemporary occupation by international forces in Afghanistan has encountered an entirely different set of circumstances and a complex set of diversified interests. Almost 2.8 billion people have suffered direct and indirect damages in South and Central Asia. Moreover, another negative byproduct of the war in Afghanistan has been the export of terrorism to some Western and Eurasian countries.

There are two sides to Afghanistan. On one hand, Afghanistan has continuously remained a cause of disagreement among the world community; on the other hand, it has been a uniting point. During the Afghan intervention by the U.S.-led International Security Assistance Force (ISAF), the conflicts of interests have greatly reduced the possibilities for success.

There are various matrixes of conflicts, and each of these sources of conflict has contributed to the broader instability. There has been interest-based competition among the international stakeholders as well as regional conflict, occurring almost on a country-by-country basis.

The worst of these conflicts was the race between Afghanistan's neighboring states, such as Pakistan, Iran and Tajikistan. Pakistan took a further step to adversely impact the broader military situation by supporting the Taliban based in Pakistan as well as Afghanistan. The role played by India and China in the reconstruction, along with their reluctance over sending troops, has also been significant.

There were also stand-offs over transportation routes in the region, which Pakistan tried to take maximum advantage of as a destabilizing factor. Meanwhile, Russia opened new troop movement corridors and facilitated new routes for transportation. This development further created more possibilities for Russia to re-integrate with the West in general, and the U.S. in particular. Linked by mutual interests, there now seems to be the possibility for future joint initiatives in the region.

An important aspect of the endgame in Afghanistan is that China and the U.S. are not on the same page on a wide range of issues. The U.S.'s primary focus in the region is creating a 'Greater Central Asia' or a 'New Silk Road' that connects almost all the potential economic zones of Asia. The disturbing point of this approach, however, is that Central Asia and Afghanistan can only connect economically with the rest of the Asia either through the ports of Karachi and Guwadar in Pakistan or through Port Abbas in Iran.

Pakistan is actively tilting towards China, while previous antagonism between Iran and the U.S. shows signs of abating. The relationship between Iran and the U.S. could improve, especially now that a liberal government has been elected in the clergy-led Persian country, which also happens to be a close ally of India.

The changing notions of security in the region due to the ISAF pullout, especially in Russia and its allied Central Asian states, will prove to be the major factor regarding the future stability of Afghanistan. Destabilizing factors like the presence of the Taliban on the Pakistani-Afghan border will pose a major threat to the interests of Russia, Central Asia, Iran, and India.

In the Russia-specific context, a number of factors play a role: the infiltration of Islamist militants throughout Eurasia, the narcotics supply from Afghanistan, the strengthened existence of Russia's ally Northern Alliance as a possible security valve, and Tajikistan's connectivity with India and the rest of the world via Port Abbas in Iran.

These connections between Afghanistan and Asia, Central Asia and Eurasia are of importance to the West. An axis of Eurasia-Iran-India with the support of the U.S. and the other Western powers is the only viable option to change the game. Pakistan has already finalized agreements with China over the construction of railways and roads to the ports of Guwadar and Karachi. This is a development that could ultimately hamper the pursuit of global interests in South Asia.

Although Russia, China, and the Central Asian states have been on the same page about Afghanistan, at least to a certain extent, their competition of economic interests has separated them into two different groups: the Shanghai Cooperation Organization (SCO) and the Collective Security Treaty Organization (CSTO).

Central Asia's socio-cultural nexus with Afghanistan would be an edge for Russia, especially from the demographic point of view. The strategic contours of this advantage can be glimpsed by watching how Russia interacts with the Northern Alliance.

In addition, by allowing the U.S. military to cross its territory after 2009, Russia now has an opening to revive its relationship with NATO and, especially, with the U.S.

The worst aspect of the current situation is that international forces have done practically nothing to root out drug production in Afghanistan, which has further aggravated the security concerns of Russia and the Central Asian states.

Moreover, Russia's aspiration for the enhanced role of the United Nations in Afghanistan during the post-ISAF pullout stage has added value and prestige. In the post-pullout scenario, the role of Russia would become crucial: Russia would be geopolitically at the helm of almost every development in Afghanistan. As a result, the prospects for new Tajik-Afghan border security measures are inevitable.

At the Chicago summit, NATO reached the decision of gradually handing over control to the Afghan local security forces. Although there is much dissension among NATO members over the successes, achievements and failures in the context of objectives and vision for the intervention, there is visible consensus among them regarding the withdrawal.

According to estimates, $4.1 billion a year are required for Afghanistan after the ISAF pullout. However, the direct and indirect costs, as well as the adverse economic impact of the war for the U.S., UK, Canada, Australia and others have probably crossed the ten-trillion-dollar mark. These high levels of monetary expenditures could have used for fighting unemployment and poverty within these countries, or at least, in the countries where poverty has become the sole reason behind the expansion of terrorism globally through terrorist syndicates.

The practical geostrategic realities suggest that the U.S. may not attain its future interests in Central-South Asia without partners in the region such as Russia, Tajikistan, India, and Iran. Banking on the Taliban would be disastrous not only for Afghanistan but also for the liberal and secular majority population of Pakistan as well. The Talibanization of

Afghanistan would ultimately influence the interdependent security of the region, especially in Pakistan.

It is assumed that Pakistan, under Nawaz Sharif, would favor an orientation towards China and Saudi Arabia. An India-Russia-Central Asia nexus would be another potential option because the state policy of ethno-sectarian exclusivity in Pakistan would never allow there a major policy change that would change its ethnically Punjabi-dominated army and its Salafi Islamic school of thought.

There is another important factor: Emerging talks about regional solutions led by China and Russia are becoming a central discussion point among Asian academics. It is therefore important for almost all international actors, particularly the U.S., to consider an integrated approach towards the ISAF pullout and Afghan security and stability thereafter.

The international community needs to make it through a difficult next stage that consists of the ISAF pullout, Afghan elections, and negotiations with the Taliban. The policy of gradual pullout is important, but chances of a gradual increase in anarchy in Afghanistan are also high, which would be the real test for the Afghan National Army and security system.

We have reached an important point.

It is now possible to consider building a new state in Afghanistan from the ethno-sectarian point of view. A sustainable peace in Afghanistan will not be possible until a localized model of Afghan federalism is developed that accommodates all ethno-linguistic and religious-sectarian demographic groups appropriately.

The most important factor would be the ability to build relationships between Afghan society and the new state. This can only be attained through transparent governance at the local level, empowerment of communities and determining the relative power of the federal authorities. Until then, the Afghan people will not be at the center of state-building or economic development.

In short, stability will remain a dream for Afghanistan until these conditions are met.

How Russia-U.S. relations play out in Afghanistan could hold the key not only for a successful exit strategy from Afghanistan, but also for a sustainable solution for future Afghan affairs.

Other options, while appearing to resolve matters in the short-term, may only end up complicating issues over the long-term.

Published in Russia Direct, Moscow on July 26, 2013

RUSSIA AMID CHANGING PERSPECTIVE OF AFGHANISTAN

The changing strategic realities after the gradual international pullout from Afghanistan will require an entirely new set of approach for the sustainability of non-extremist governance and stability of social fabric. Amid, such an unpredictable future of war-game stage of Central and South Asia, Russia is one of potential players that can come forward to discuss new matrix of long-term building of state structure in Afghanistan. This requires an out of traditional box of security engagement paradigm and demands an integrated approach for the broader re-coordination of diversified interests.

Afghanistan has been the centre of conflicts among world powers since at least lat two centuries, and if seen in the perspective of global security and Asian composite, it has been a major centre of international disorder causing political-strategic upheavals on the world stage. Being located at an incredible strategic place, it has gone through the various waves of destructions, on the debris of which world now is attempting the reconstruction that suits the various interests.

Since the world power have decided a gradual withdrawal from Afghanistan in 2014, the issue is gaining further importance as almost whole developed and developing world has engaged their stakes into the war torn country. In these highly crucial moments for Afghanistan, the neighboring world powers are pushing forward for copping the new emerging challenges concerning their interests that are associated with the stability in Afghanistan. The history attached to the Afghan war theatre is highly discussed globally; hence, it is important to think now about post ISAF pullout.

All roads cross through Afghanistan

Afghanistan is the strategic heart of Asia, a kind of Suez Canal that can potentially connect almost all economic regions of the continent.

This is the main reason along with so many others that international interests have been attempting and struggling for their presence and outreach there. It is also one of the important most sources of the much hounded energy resources.

Russia – Afghanistan relations have remained on the positive note since the period of Tzar, which further developed into better ties after the October revolution. Being a historical partner of Afghanistan, writes Monika Pawar in her article 'Russia's Afghan Strategy: What are its Interests?' "Russia will have to keep a check on formidable economic rivals in Afghanistan like (the one) China." It has to deal with four matrixes of regional interests simultaneously: Pakistan and its backing by the Arab Salafism; Shanghai Cooperation Organization (SCO); India-Iran-Tajikistan trimetric and the West. It is the matter of higher playing field for Russia that in the context of American notion of the Greater Central-and-South Asia, how its re-coordinates its interests in a manner that interests of majority stakeholders are not challenged. Besides, what possible role it could play in the state formation and development of Afghanistan and stability of Afghan people would materially mean a lot in terms of strengthening sustainable stability in Afghanistan as well as in the region.

Eurasian interests

The strategic niche of the Russia and the Central Asian States is interdependent; therefore, their multilateral and collective engagement for the interests cannot be avoided. There are at least four key cornerstones of Eurasian concerns about the post international pullout scenario, which include possibility of Taliban takeover of Kabul may reduce the presence of Northern Alliance in the Afghan affairs that ultimately would lead Eurasian countries to have an easy access to the Indian Ocean through Iran. Besides, there is an undeniable security concerns regarding the infiltration of Islamist militants in the Eurasia. The most important would be the thin chances for access to the natural resources in the Pashtun provinces of Afghanistan. In addition, the highly important one is the narcotics supply. The civil war or dominating armed conflicts are not in the favor of Russia, Central Asia and the West.

According to Ekaterina Stepanova's research work, UN Office on Drugs and Crime (UNODC) reports that in 2006 the share of Afghan opiates passing through the Northern route was less than 15 percent of the total, while more traditional routes were more heavily utilized (53 percent through Iran and 33 percent through Pakistan). The share of heroin in Russia's opiate consumption has also marginally declined.

Afghanistan is of key significance to Russia's wider Central Asian policy and its claim to a great power status, writes Monika Pawar. "Moreover, the socio-cultural and ethno-linguistic nexus between non-Pashtun Afghanistan and the Central Asian Countries that creates friendly cushion for Russia and its allied in Central Asia in Afghanistan. The support of Central Asian countries and Russia to the Northern Alliance, an alliance of Tajiks, Uzbeks and Turkmen against the Taliban, is borne out of this socio-cultural affinity.

It is therefore a greater opportunity for Russia to further its and allies strategic goals in Afghanistan, as the new Afghan situation is much different than that of during Soviet year, not only in terms of global fabric of politics but also in the context of Afghanistan's internal realities and demographic tilts."

One of the major and bold strategic steps by Russia was opening the transportation rout for NATO after July 2009, when Pakistan asserted its strategic importance by disallowing NATO supply from its territory. This would ultimately open up a new chapter of Russian foreign policy approach towards the West.

Russia has also been focusing the strengthening of the security system. According to an analytical write up of Andrei Akulov it is strengthening the "security system in the strategic southern area, including its military component, emphasizing the need for close cooperation with fellow members of regional security alliances." On the other hand, Russian approach regarding enhanced role of United Nations in Afghanistan after ISAF pullout has also a shared context with the rest of stakeholders. It is not doubt; Russia should do every possible effort to avert possible instability at its borders in the changing scene of the game.

Collective Approach

Afghanistan needs a collective or an integrated approach by almost all stakeholders. While considering in the Russian or Eurasian context, it becomes essentials that how Russia and the Central Asia manage together a viable engagement with the other competing interests to carry forward the continuous and in-depth reconstruction of not only physical landscape of Afghanistan but essentially the state-building and specifically the sociologically an ethno-linguistic reconstruction. This can only be possible through the developing a consensus among and between regional and international stakeholders. This the point, where Russia can become a real sense bridge between the West and the Asian actors that have avoidable differences, and couch-able competition. This primarily will require understanding that Afghanistan is a demographic entity in its own.

Besides, the fallacies like that almost all Pashtun are pro-Pakistan or Pakistan friendly Taliban needs to be washed away. This Afghan transition could be an ideal moment for connecting the pieces in Afghanistan vertically and horizontally. Russia has created a new set of the relations with Europe and North America by cushioning route facilitation for NATO and other similar initiatives; it already enjoys the historical friendly relations with India, which itself is an old ally of Iran and has deeper engagement with Tajikistan; and finally has no adverse relations with China. Therefore it may be in the greater interests of Russia to engage with all international stakeholders particularly US and India (and China as well) for the continuous reconstruction of Afghanistan from the state, society and development point of view and ensure the strategic sidelining of Taliban and the similar rouge elements from Afghan scene.

Reconstruction

It is already too late. The downpour of global monitory resources in Afghanistan has failed to prove as a stability-creating agent. It neither has helped resolve the Afghan issue, nor has channeled up the new development flow. At least there have been no remarkable gain in the minimizing the size of populace that lives bellow the line of poverty in millions. Such a huge investment of trillions of dollars could have been utilized for the eradication of poverty that is mother of all terrorism in the world.

Much has been discussed about Afghanistan in the terms of various interest groups. This the time when a new discussion and decisions needs to be taken for the viable federal statehood in Afghanistan that accommodates ethno-linguistic and sectarian plurality. Until and unless appropriately consensual three-tier mechanism of federal state structure is not created on the ethno-linguistic line and Afghan people at various tiers are not being given the representation after the due and necessary empowerment, the threats of instability and destabilization would always loom large over the region.

Since majority of the Afghanistan population is liberal or secular, there is a need to find missing links where this fabric is challenged by the extremists and destabilizing factors. It is no doubt a global failure that it has not started the reconstruction of Afghanistan and its state from ethno-social perspective, which unfortunately does not devise the balanced demographic chemistry of a viable and sustainable statehood. Besides, it is important to focus on the role of United Nations in such kind of global interventions. The issue of Afghanistan has many aspects but essentially, from the structural point of view it is the issue of appropriate ethnic accommodation in the state field there.

A similar situation is also prevailing in Pakistan, where dominancy of ethnic Punjabi in association with Urdu-speaking privileged community has perverted society in name of Islamization so that Punjab may carry on its colonization of Sindh, Baluchistan, and KP in Pakistan. It is also important to note here that in so many manners, if the chemistry of statecraft Pakistan is not changed, the issue of Afghanistan will never get resolved. Mostly because, the exclusive and non-representative security establishment of Pakistan devises it's foreign policy, which ultimately is dominated by ethnic Punjabis and their junior partner Urdu speaking bureaucracy. Therefore, it is also essential to find the Afghan destabilization strings within the single ethnic dominated and non-pluralistic state chemistry in Pakistan. In the long term perspective, it is therefore would become unavoidable that after an optimum level stability in Afghanistan, a much needed state-chemistry change of Pakistan will also be needed. Until and unless Pakistan is not made free from ethnic Punjabi-cum Urdu and Salafi minority dominancy, there are no signs of major policy change of Pakistan towards the stability of Central-South Asian region.

Published on the website of Russian Council on International Affairs

CAUTIOUSNESS IN AFGHANISTAN-PAKISTAN PARTNERSHIP

In a recent meeting between President Asraf Ghani and Prime Minister Nawaz Sharif, Afghanistan and Pakistan have reached over an understanding on the security cooperation, capacity building and mutual trade. This unexpected development exclusively includes the training of Afghan National Army by Pakistan Army.

In so many manners, this out of blue development between both of the conflicting countries can be read in the versatile even and odd meanings for the impacts on the future statehood and statecraft of Afghanistan. The cooperation between two conflicting countries is always considered a good omen; however sometimes it buzzes alarms when probabilities and possibilities of long term irreversible impacts out of these developments become inevitable.

A cautious moment

Afghanistan and the engaged world is need to step forwardly cautiously whenever the process of Afghan security establishment development and capacity building is initiated. The Afghanistan-Pakistan understanding may serve two immediate interests of Afghanistan -- the limited gains from import and export, and submissiveness of Pakistan supported Taliban. It is bound to leave, on the other hand, long term adverse impacts on Afghanistan's internal governance and statecraft because of the historical characteristic of Pakistan Army.

Pakistan Army in its origin is an oligarchy of ethnic monotony. It has carried forward the colonial legacy in an uglier manner by massacring its own people in Sindh and Balochistan; have been instrumental in training the religious extremists for the proxy wars; and have been overthrowing democratically elected governments unto recent past. Thus, Pakistan Army is the sole reason for thrashing Pakistan to the verge of collapse.

Afghan National Army as well as Afghanistan's security establishment, if trained by Pakistan Army, may get same viral epidemics inherited by Pakistani military establishment. It seems if Afghanistan and Pakistan agree on the military cooperation, later is bound to see military rules in future together with the inter-establishment ethno-linguist and sectarian fragmentation and conflicts. There are always possibilities that Pakistan Army's role in Afghanistan will also give a cushion to the Pakistani influence and infiltration within the Afghan security establishment and governance.

A new great game

If Afghanistan and Pakistan agree on the capacity building of the Afghan Army, possibilities of a new 'great game' may increase in Afghanistan on the lines of fragmentation and internal conflicts within the state. Afghanistan may possibly get out of the destabilization caused by the proxy Islamists for sometime through its military agreement with Pakistan, but it most probably would repeat back its previous history in which coups, counter-coups, split as well as factionalism on the ethnic and sectarian lines may arise. This exclusively pose threat of a new phase of Afghanistan insecurity in which various internal and external factors may play with Afghanistan security establishment according to their interests and give birth to decades of state fragmentation on the land of already war-fatigue Afghans.

What actually needs to be done?

The world needs to develop a particular model for the development and capacity enhancement of Afghanistan state, particularly its security establishment and more specifically its military. An appropriate way may be that the world powers that have been engaged in Afghanistan since last one decade should form a joint pool of military and security fraternity for the capacity building and training. Such a collective or joint pool would not only develop Afghanistan's security establishment in a highly competitive manner but also give engaged powers to club together their specialties for the state building around the world whenever and wherever an Afghanistan like situation arise. This will also give a great space to Afghanistan for engaging with the world at a broader level so that it may further strength its future security and stability.

Published on the website of Russian Council on International Affairs

SOCIAL MOVEMENTS: WHERE DOES SINDH STAND IN THE WORLD?

'Peacefulness' was a diplomatic phrase, if not a jargon, of the twentieth century – a time when 'world' was not transformed into a conscious and highly connected 'globe'. The bent of international and regional actors towards engaging with the peaceful and violent movements can simplistically but truly termed as political and strategic hypocrisy. How the world today positions itself towards peaceful social and political movements? A ten-million dollar question, indeed!

One can react while reading this unfashionable term of 'political and strategic hypocrisy'; however, it is very simple of understand. An interest based tagging for the legitimacy of violent and illegitimacy of peaceful movements. If seen in the perspective of international community's approach towards different political and social movements, the wishful tagging of the terms like 'peaceful', 'non-violent' or the 'violent' becomes a phenomenal disposition of the interest based approach. One can conclude that there is a conflict of approaches in the world – interest based versus justice based. In many a cases, interest based approach has been adopted repeatedly by the various states and powers. Meanwhile, justice based approach is paradoxically owned by the peoples. Numerous movements in the various continents have been encountering this phenomenal dilemma.

There are at least three significant sets of the major social and political movements in the world – slow-paced movements around socio-economic justice; the Arab-spring style movement for the democratic governance; and the movements for the territorial liberation.

Most of the movements based on socio-economic justice have an outlook of the structural and legal reforms for the socio-economic justice for the women, transgender and marginalized sections of the societies; hence they are not only peaceful but also are supported by the governments as well as international forums. No government bothers thinking their tagging in terms of peaceful or violent. They mostly are catered through the international development funds, which are pipelined via international development aid programs of various developed countries as well as international and regional financial interest groups and bodies of various socio-political outfits.

The Arab Spring style movements have been both peaceful and violent simultaneously; and the majority among the international community has never shown their concern about their being peaceful or violence. This is what we can say strategic hypocrisy where the principle of peacefulness is sidelined over the niche of interests.

The victim most of the socio-political movements are of the territorial liberation in the various parts of the world, which have always gathered this typical fuss of jargonized terms of 'violent' versus 'peaceful'. No doubt, most of the freedom movements around the world are violent; however, the hypocrisy of the world community becomes extraordinarily visible when they start measuring and considering the issues. They, hitherto, only have prioritized the violent movements over the peaceful ones. The case of Palestine, Kosovo, Kurdistan, and Tamil Elam has always attracted focus of not only the various countries but also of the regional forums like European Union and Arab League as well as various bodies of the United Nations. Kashmir does not fall in this category, although there is an oldest UN resolution regarding it. Kashmir can be set out of the matrix because the violence acknowledge and attributed with Kashmir has been based on non-Kashmiri Jihadists from the Punjab province of Pakistan. Contrary to this, there is at least one highly populist and massive movement for the freedom and self-determination of Sindh in Pakistan, which is very little known to the world outside despite the fact that the movement dates back to the movement for the liberation of Bangladesh.

There is a highly power high scale insurgency and war in Balochistan, and no doubt, it has been successful to attain international attention. Since Baloch are around six million in the hilly and mountainous province forming sixty percent area of Pakistan, therefore they are unable to make a pressurizing public outpour; hence expecting a peaceful movement in Balochistan is out of question.

If one reviews Sindhi newspapers of the last sixty-nine years, one surprises to see that this homeland of 50 million Sindhis have never been silent. Activism and movement building in the form of hunger strikes, protest sit-ins, inter and intra cities on-foot marches, rallies, shutter down strikes and vehicular jam strikes has always occupied the newspapers. However, Sindhi uprising during last five years has not only been exceptional but phenomenal as well.

In 2008, a Sindhi nationalist party Jeay Sindh Qomi Mahaz (JSQM) held Sindh Freedom March in almost every district of Sindh, which was attended by thousands of the people. On November 7, 2009, on the party's call for Sindh Freedom March, at least 2.5 hundred thousand people gathered in the city and demanded the world powers and the United Nations an independent and sovereign status, in which British invaded it in 1843. Invasion of Sindh in 1843 was a violation of various treaties between the Emirs of Sindh and Royal deputies of the Great Britain.

On March 23, 2012, JSQM again held a Sindh Freedom March attended by two million Sindhis. Talking to the 'Freedom March' JSQM leader Bashir Qureshi announced Sindh bidding farewell the historical Resolution of Pakistan that was adopted on March 23, 1940. He also sought international community's help in this regard. He was killed through poison on April 8, 2012.

On March 23, 2014, JSQM again organized 'Sindh Freedom March' in Karachi. At least five million people according to the various international and Sindh based print and electronic media houses. To pressurize JSQM for cancelation of the Freedom March, the top leader of the JSQM and brother of Bashir Qureshi, Maqsood Qureshi was gunned down and later on burnt down to the ashes by the "security agencies of Pakistan." According to the JSQM leadership, they were already under pressure by the state agencies asking them to cancel the Freedom March. While addressing the mammoth gathering, JSQM Chairperson Sunan Qureshi demanded United Nations, the USA, UK, France, Russia, and China for their intervention and support for the independence of Sindh. Unlike some portions of Western, Middle East and Afghan media, the news found no space in South Asian media.

The overall trend and the tilt of ignorance and negligence by the media, governments and to certain extent international forums toward this peaceful movement of South Asia would one day possibly push them to become violent. A neglected and underestimated highly popular peaceful movement usually turns into the violent one.

It is quit convincing that under-estimating a peaceful popular movement would mean that world has no space for the peaceful movements, hence a highly peaceful movement may possibly turn into the violent one.

Despite apparently professing peace and non-violence agenda around the globe, the political and strategic hypocrisy by the world powers regarding movement of Sindh will add up into chaos in the South Asia. This is the prime opportunity, when the world by focusing a peaceful movement can set an example that international community prefers peaceful socio-political movements to the radical and violent one.

Let the world set at least first example to prioritize this peaceful movement before it is too late. The time has come, when the world community needs to avoid political and strategic hypocrisy and set example for the world politics of dissenting social movements.

Published in Daily Afghanistan Times, Kabul on April 13, 201

POST SCOTLAND REFERENDUM FREEDOM MOVEMENTS

United Kingdom, like its historical contribution in the socio-political development of its previous colonies in Asia, Africa, Australia, and North America, has recently proved to be a leading trend setter by holding historical referendum in Scotland to seek their will for either union or secession.

Such a noble act was previously carried out by Canada that gave Quebec an opportunity to express their will in 1980 and later on again in 1995. Recently Spain has carried referendum in the federating state of Catalonia, in which unlike Quebec and Scotland, Catalonia voted 81 percent in the favor of secession. Whether the will of Catalonian would be materialized or they would engage with the Spain for more autonomy and benefits? Ultimately in both of the situations Catalonian people will be the beneficiaries.

In brief, the bold and highly democratic action by the UK has ultimately left impacts on the federating countries around the world, where ethnic-nationalism has acquired highly legitimate space as well as strength.

Federations in the crises

Many of the federations in the world are historical, some are not only very recent but also have developed on the illegitimate foundations, therefore have caused ethnic monopolies of dominant ethnic –nations and federating states over the rest.

Some highly recognized freedom movements among the federating countries in the world are still yearning for the materialization of their collective will. Some federations have already resolved the issues of secessionist movements either completely or to greater extent that include a typical example of Corsica in France, which is now a cohesive part of the French federation. It also include the example of Chechnya, where freedom movement was in booms during last decades; however under President Putin the Chechnya has pressed for the integration within the federation. Another example is of Kashmir, which due to policies of Nehru is a part of India and enjoys greater autonomy. Hence if infiltration of non-Kashmiri Jihadist ends from outside, there would be no significant secessionism there and violence would finally recede.

Existing secessionist movements

There are some prominent legitimate secessionist or freedom movements in Asia that include Tibet in China, Kurdistan in Iraq and Turkey, Sindh and Balochistan in Pakistan. Among these, Tibet is an entirely different case in which unlike India's autonomy giving space to Kashmir, successor Chinese leadership particularly Deng Xiao Peng snatched agreed autonomy from Tibetan that Dalai Lama and Mao Zedong reached upon by the mid of the last century. Kurdistan in Turkey is undergoing the reformist process in which Turkey due to pressure from USA and EU is trying to recognize legitimate rights of Kurds and is also attempting to give them more agency. Kurdistan in Iraq is almost autonomous now and have a semi-freedom status; however it seems that they would win freedom in the post ISIS phenomenon. Sindh and Balochistan were annexed with a non-historical federation of Pakistan against their will in 1947. The foundation of Hindu and Muslim nations on which Pakistan was created out of India proved failure in 1971 when Pakistani federating state East Bengal became Bangladesh on the ethnic-nation lines.

Where referendum is meaningless

Pakistan is country where democracy has not got an entry as yet. Half life of Pakistan's sixty-seven years has remained under military rule. Rest of half has witnessed election frauds. The provincial assemblies of Sindh, Balochistan and Khyber Pakhtunkhuwa are not free to run their business as their business is monitored by the military related intelligence agencies that usually check the agenda of these assemblies before their legislative sessions. Besides, because Sindh and Balochistan were annexed with Pakistan unwillingly and Khyber Pakhtunkhuwa (KP) became part of Pakistan on the basis of Britain's lease of KP according to Durand Line agreement, referendum for the Sindh and Balochistan by Pakistan would be an inappropriate instrument. Nor the provincial assemblies in Pakistan are autonomous enough to pass the resolution for secession from the federations. In a very recent move, Provincial Assembly Sindh has passed a resolution on December 10, 2014 demanding Federation of Pakistan to practically materialize the provincial autonomy given through XVIII constitutional amendment five years ago or be ready for the dismantling of the Federation.

What then?

In such situations, the role of international community and the United Nations (UN) become pivotal. Either the referendum in these provinces should be carried by UN or international community should think of other means in this regards. The role and historical responsibility of the UK in this regards becomes of importance.

Besides, UN itself needs to legislate regarding the secession or freedom movements in the federations around the world.

Published in Daily Afghanistan Times, Kabul on December 13, 2014

THE GLOBAL SECURITY CHALLENGE FROM AFGHANISTAN TO UKRAINE

Issues of security and stability in Asia and Europe are interdependent. Given the continual rise of new conflicts from Asia-Pacific to the Atlantic, these issues and conflicts need to be addressed through a fundamentally new approach to security.

We are now witnessing the outbreak and intensification of conflicts across the world, from Afghanistan to Ukraine. Major 21st century conflicts have not yet appropriately concluded in Afghanistan, Iraq and the Middle East. Ukraine now risks destabilizing the global security architecture that has existed since the Cold War. These conflicts have not only shaken the very foundations of continental and regional security and stability but also the overall international security regime.

Underneath the inter-state antagonism is a second layer of issues and conflicts, most of which are of an intra-state nature that play (or may potentially play) a crucial role in the overall global security environment. These intra-state conflicts have also left decisive impacts on the stability of the conflicting state-parties. This group of conflicts and issues include the secessionist movements of Kurdistan in Iraq; Tibet in China; Sindh and Balochistan in Pakistan; the Salafist movements in Syria and Iraq; and tensions between Pakistan and Afghanistan.

Both historically and contemporarily, the Middle East has witnessed two categories of broader conflicts – Arab versus Ajam (non-Arab Turks, Kurds, and Iranians), and Salafi versus Sunni and Shia. In South Asia, the Britain occupied the sovereign countries of Sindh and Balochistan in 1843 and 1854, respectively, in a bid to invade Afghanistan. Tibet until the middle of the twentieth century was an independent country; however, after Mao Tse-tung's revolution, Tibet became part of China in 1950. Despite Mao assuring the Dalai Lama of complete autonomy for Tibet through an agreement, China continues to dominate the political future of Tibet.

These contemporary international security challenges are unavoidably dependent on the social and power dynamics of the conflict zones. Hence, addressing these in accordance with their own dynamism as well as with an integrated approach would be the only way forward for their sustainable resolution. The results of the military interventions in Iraq and Afghanistan, as well as the outcomes of the faded Arab Spring, are the same. Meanwhile, the issues of Kurdistan, Tibet, Sindh and Balochistan – not to mention the Israeli-Palestinian conflict – remain unresolved even after six decades. The strategic posturing on the Korean peninsula still commands a central role in the security of the Pacific region around China.

This on-again, off-again nature of the conflicts in Asia has engulfed the security, stability and economic future of not only Asia, but also the Euro-Atlantic nations. There is a need for consensus between the U.S., Russia and the European Union on their foreign policy approaches when it comes to Asia. There needs to be a positive disposition of the core issues of Asia that have become the tectonic plates of conflict in the modern world.

We need a new way of thinking about security and stability in the world. The way forward would include:

First, strengthen Afghanistan through appropriate state building and social development measures enough so that it may become protected socio-politically and territorially from neighboring countries. This requires consensus between and among the Euro-Atlantic nations, Russia, the Central Asian nations, Iran and India before any final solution exists.

Second, resolve the issue of the Kurds in Iraq and Turkey, which, for decades, have been the primary stage for the Kurdistan movement. Turks and Kurds are engaged now in a resolution due to pressure mounted on both sides by the EU nations by organizations such as the Kurdistan Workers' Party (PKK). Meanwhile, the creation of Kurdistan out of Iraq has now become viable after Daish terrorism in Iraq, since the creation of a new Ajam state in the Middle East would also be a strategic check on the growing threat of Salafist challenges.

Third, consider a combined Israeli-Palestinian state as a possible option in which Palestinians are constitutionally and practically granted autonomy and security.

Fourth, dismantle the infrastructure and strategic safe havens of the Salafist terrorist groups in Pakistan. Since the political structure in Pakistan is still a complex patchwork quilt of authorities, this can only be done through the creation of one sovereign state (Sindh-Balochistan) or two separate states. In this case, the Khyber Pakhtunkhuwa province of Pakistan would possibly be annexed to Afghanistan. This would also resist the threat of nuclear instability from Pakistan.

Fifth, devise a solution of the Tibetan issue in which the will of the Tibetan people is first and foremost. The role played by India in this regard would be crucial.

Sixth, a solution, agreeable to all stakeholders, specifically including the Ukrainian separatists, Russia, the states of Europe bordering Ukraine (including those in Scandinavia) would guarantee a broader sustenance of peace in Eurasia.

Until these fundamentals of global security are understood and addressed appropriately, broader security and stability among Asian and Euro-Atlantic nations will be impossible.

Published in Russia Direct, Moscow on September 9, 2014

III
COLONIAL STATE AND SOCIETY

OF STATE AND SOCIETY

Human society has two inherent permanent features and tendencies—the emergence of social-waves and the process of structuralisation in those social-waves. This opposition is a chain of causalities, containing the manifestation of dynamics in the political economy and social progress, as well as their retrogression and social stagnation. No phenomenon of social movements around the globe, particularly in the previous colonies, is an exception to this dialectic of mass expression.

State v society

Human history has witnessed and undergone this process through the structuralisation of movements, religions, ideologies and revolutions. It has left long-lasting imprints on social institutions, particularly the mega-social organism of the state, and on the process of state building and state formation.

The contemporary crises of state versus society and the liberty of the individual versus the state's reckless vigilance using the excuse of national security have deep roots in this fundamental dynamic and dialectic of broader social behavior.

The widening gap between states and societies during the process of globalization is at a highly naïve stage in developed countries, if compared with the developing and underdeveloped world. In other words, state-society frictions in the global north and south have not only their own peculiarities but also variant degrees and velocities of social processes. This is further visible in the polar opposite nature of statehood between the previous colonies and their colonizers.

Besides, on the debris of the state apparatus in previous colonies and colonizers, there have emerged the contemporary virtual forms of soft-colonization, which no doubt is at the height of neo-colonialism and semi-colonialism. This has highly peculiar connotations in ethnolinguistically diverse societies, countries and their arc of class-cum-federal structures.

The impacts of colonization on the polity, state-building and state-society relations in previous colonies and their colonizers are evident. Today's virtual colonialism has even worse aspects to this. Thus, the understanding of state-society relations in the global south, particularly in the previous colonies, in the perspective of contemporary politics and social movement would lead to another stage of discourse. Nevertheless, an analysis of the contemporary state-society relations would hardly re-direct to the hidden depths if the 'structuralism' versus 'social-wave' dynamics is not at the core of broader discourse.

Almost all religions, practical manifestations of political doctrines, movements, and cultural ethos become dogma once swamped in structuralisation. The institutions of mullahism, priesthood and panditism, political leadership cults, party dictatorship and thinking stereotypes are common examples.

Colonial state formation

State building and state formation are two different aspects of statehood. State building is a process in which the state evolves out of society through gradual evolution whilst state formation is a process where state construction takes place in a non-traditional manner, based mostly on an extraordinary centralized statehood. State formation in most cases involves the role of external factors in the embryology of the state apparatus.

In the process of state formation, peculiar courses of political actions take place, where particular state elements acquire bigger roles or powers (non-traditionally, if not abnormally) in comparison with others in statecraft.

The formation of a colonial state has historically been aimed at providing a buffer between the colonizers and their subjects. This was attained through creating a class of bureaucrats, sallariat (salaried middle class) and the establishment of various forms of rural-lordships.

The contribution of colonizers in terms of political discourse and culture has helped colonial societies to grow. However, it has meant to regulate relations between colonizers and colonies, mostly in the colonizer's interest. This led, for example, to the previous British colonies wearing a new sociality—a reversal of the previous socio-economic relations. Undivided India is a highly intelligible model of studies for that. India underwent social engineering by the British Raj, which created permanent frictions and upheavals, despite the fact that these are at the heart of development dynamics in South Asia.

The legacy of colonialism has sprung a new course of socio-political metabolism. The independence of colonies, therefore, have gradually and continuously undergone the process of the post-colonial state versus society, the neo-colonial state versus society and internal-colonial or semi-colonial state versus native or internal semi-colonies.

Freedom and the state

If post-British withdrawal from Southasia is deeply analyzed, it will show a peculiar course of state-formation, social progress and consequently, state society conflicts.

If seen in the post-British withdrawal context, various states have undergone an exclusive path to contain the state's classical role of maintaining minimum civil conditions for the citizenry to avail of a free and peaceful life. In so many manners, the state's legitimacy over the use of violence has either been over-used, as in Myanmar and Sri Lanka, or this legitimacy has been shared with state-sponsored extremists, as with the urban terrorists in Pakistan.

The exclusive takeover of the polity and the state apparatus by the particular classes of India after 1947 still carries the strings of colonial statehood, if seen in a state-society perspective. Pakistan has undergone an uneven course of militarization of the state as well as some selective societal groups. Sri Lanka has taken various courses of state retrogression in which state-society relations have been antagonized through a repressive order where harmony has been compromised over the prioritization of the ethnic interest between the Tamil and Sinhala people.

Besides, the state has translated itself gradually into militarization, where minimum civil conditions have always been at the stake. Even Nepal, always proud for never being colonized, has remained under a virtual colonial status since the British occupation of India. Myanmar has become the worst example of a military's dominance over the state apparatus, which turned society retrogressive. Bhutan, like Nepal, is facing the drawbacks of being a land-locked geo-political entity. Maldives, and to certain extent Nepal and Bhutan, has turned itself into a state of convenience in terms of its foreign policy, which ultimately has fall-outs in its own societies and the interests of friendly neighbors. Bangladesh, unlike others, has started cleansing house to detach the impacts, adversaries and strings of Muslim terrorism and war crimes committed by Pakistan in 1971.

Southasian states, naturally, underwent the process of transition after independence from British rule. The state apparatus left behind by the British as an institutional legacy was not only a Southasian adaptation of the Western statehood of its time but was also structured to serve colonial interests and prolong colonial rule. The unexpected withdrawal of the British from Southasia due to World War II left no room to transform the nature of the state apparatus from colonization into a real republic.

The states in Southasia are still structured to serve global powers, in comparison with the interests of their own citizens. In the absence of 'real' colonizers, the role of colonizers has been taken over by civil and military elites. This has squared the level of alienation among the people vis-à-vis the state.

Since most Southasian countries constitute a united diversity, they are reluctant for social movements that lead to a transformation of the state and for the judicious distribution of power vertically and horizontally. Empowerment and development in Southasia is, therefore, conditioned on the judicious distribution of power among ethnicities, classes, communities and sects. Besides, the colonizer's leftover state apparatus legacy is the major reason behind the unending conflicts, underdevelopment and militarization in the region.

If summed up, the transition of Southasian states from colonial into postcolonial states, neocolonial arrangements and semi-colonial as well as internal colonial states has always been the fault on which politics and development in Southasia has been directed and redirected through certain classes, portions of the states apparatus, elitist mindset and structural cultures of the state-society dynamics.

The writer is a Sindhi refugee activist and journalist, currently staying in New Delhi, India.

Published in daily The Kathmandu Post on March 16, 2014

COLONISED INTERNALLY

The boom of socialist politics in the global order between 1950-1970s, the Cold War episode that played out in Afghanistan during the 1980s and the 'war on terror' during the 2000s have been instrumental in state development, social progress, economic growth and the political narrative of Southasia. These global conflicts for power and resources have always been an external factor behind the gap in between states and societies.

After the British withdrawal, Southasian states needed a new state apparatus as the old ones were built to serve the interests of external colonizers. But the continuation of the colonial legacy of the state apparatus created local and internal colonizers who preferred to collaborate with external post-colonial and neo-colonial elements instead of redirecting progress and development to the people.

Due to the much-touted contest between the so-called socialist and capitalist blocks during the 1950-80s, the governments in India, Pakistan, Sri Lanka, Myanmar, Nepal, Bhutan and the Maldives could not bridge the gaps between the state and society by transforming the colonial, aristocratic and monarchial natures of their respective state oligarchies into a localized one.

Internal colonization

In some of the previous colonies in Asia and Africa, the withdrawal of colonizers created an ethno-linguistic, racial, and/or sectarian hegemony and oligarchy over the rest of the citizenry, especially by transferring state powers to selective or loyal ethno-linguistic and religious groups. South Africa, Indonesia and Pakistan have been typical examples of this.

A federation of previously sovereign and independent countries, Pakistan is a typical case study for internally colonized states. State formation in Pakistan has been a classic hegemony of ethnic Punjabis in association with the cultural, political and economic partnership of the Urdu-speaking elite over the rest of the federated provinces. Due to the

Punjabisation of Pakistan's military, civil, non-governmental and non-state elements of power, East Pakistan waged a freedom war and emerged as Bangladesh on the world map.

The Pakistani state had tried to accommodate a thin margin of Pashtuns in anti-Soviet campaigns with the support of the US. And it has internally colonized Sindh and Balochistan by accommodating the Urdu ethnic minority in Karachi city. This has resulted in a popular liberation movement, a low intensity insurgency in Sindh and highly intense warfare in Balochistan provinces. It is worth mentioning here that Sindh is the richest land in Southasia in terms of natural resources like oil, coal and methane gas.

Contemporary discontent

Globalization has attached virtual wings to the state apparatus across the globe to fly uninterrupted in comparison to society. It has undermined the previous discourse of the gradual reduction in the role of state in societal affairs.

Technological advancements associated with global connectivity have limited the domain of individual liberties, privacy and movements within and across the nation-states. The worst impact of today's state-oriented globalization, in association with the globalised security doctrines and practices combined with the widening state-society gap, has been pushing the previous colonies to choose between orderly anarchy and result-oriented social movements and transformation.

In fact, the state structures in the previous colonies have become extra-ordinarily advanced and globalised in comparison to their own societies. This phenomenon is exclusive in locally-colonized federations, where federating states/provinces and their ethnic-nations are at odds with the centre or the dominant ethnic groups.

The technology transfer to Pakistan by the West during the last four decades has been misused for the ethnic cleansing of Sindhis and Balochs. The recent unearthing of mass graves in Balochistan and extra-judicial killings in Sindh by security agencies are highly visible evidences of such misuse. It is roughly estimated that the state, as well as state-sponsored mullahs and urban terrorists, have killed around 50,000 commoners so far in Sindh and Balochistan since 2000.

Global linkages

The states of the previous colonies are becoming highly intolerant of social movements, overall rights regimes and individual liberties. The persecution of human rights activists and journalists, the censorship of movies and books, disallowing urban life, limiting freedom for women, attempting to accommodate social movements through structural transformation into failed models are some of the most notable examples. The worst situation can be observed in internally-colonized federations like Pakistan.

Since the people of these countries are in a dilemma of a peculiar kind, in which previous colonizers and neo-imperialists have played key roles, it is necessary that the people from previous colonial and neo-colonial powers come together to raise issues of common concern.

Perversion, dictatorships, local colonies and unnecessary interference of the state apparatus in societies have wrecked havoc in countries like Pakistan.

The time has come for the people of Commonwealth states, of the US and Europe in particular, to step up for real liberation and the development of people in the previous colonies so that states are kept in legitimate brackets, like in countries such as Pakistan.

It is strange that social movements, political rights and civil liberties of the developed and global north societies are highly dependent on the liberation and political salvation of societies in the previous colonies and the Global South. Let the people of previous colonies, particularly internal colonies like Sindh and Balochistan be given moral support in their battle for justice. Proper understanding, will and passion is all that is required to create connectivity for the collectivism of efforts to promote justice.

Besides, studies concerning social movements and civil liberties also need to focus on the process of social-waves versus the structurisation of human institutions. No phenomena in the human history of social progress and spiritual development combined with the relation between 'Being' (man) and 'Absolute Being' (nature) have surpassed this fundamental dynamics of human development.

Let us work out the dialectics of humanism for a better harvest of global citizenry, including poor classes and nations in chains around the world.

Published in Daily The Kathmandu Post, Nepal on March 30, 2014

IV

TRANSFORMATION

INTERNATIONAL POLITICS OF MIDDLE PATH

Geographical irritants like highly distant location from the rest of the countries, value based interests and historical setbacks are the factors behind the re-writing and re-defining the international relations, and thereby diplomacy of Japan, Australia and Sweden. They have their peculiar perspectives of not only protecting their interests but also the foreign policy exceptions like containing values of maximum restrain by Japan; extensive and exhaustive but accommodative engagement with the international community by Australia on the basis of bilateral and multilateral interests; an century long attempt to maintain neutrality by disassociating from the military alliances by Sweden.

Besides, the three countries have also played a significant role in development and rights regime support in Asia and Africa. There is also criticism however regarding the other aspects of their foreign policies, but the overall outlook and policy framework of these three countries is highly peculiar. Can these peculiarities offer more to the world? What benefits the nations and the citizens around the world can take if their roles become more comprehensive? We need to look briefly in the context.

Policy of Middle Path

If we appropriately name the foreign policy peculiarities and exceptionalism by Australia, Japan and Sweden we would justifiably name it the foreign policy of middle path, although the demanding 'national interests' have always created rough sailing for these countries to choose between interests niche and the historical matrix of their international relations.

Unlike Sweden and Japan, Australia is a NATO ally but its overall performance in the recent Afghan war was lesser prone to the criticism. Besides, the Australian support in the international development directly or through the United Nations mechanisms is an integral part of its softer engagements.

Japan, meanwhile facing security threats in the Asia-pacific, had been facing highly rudderless journey. Despite several upside-downs in its journey towards appropriation for its international engagements, Japan has corrected its course in recent years. The results of which are highly visible under Abe regime.

Sweden, unlike both have a long foreign policy history of maintaining neutrality although at various stages it has been in the hard waters in selecting neutrality over the partiality in the international engagements but its overall policy framework again has remained a real mid-path due to its continuous attempts for sticking to the neutrality.

Realism behind the 'Middle Path Exceptionalism'

The middle path policy realism behind these countries' international relations and foreign policies has some geo-political contexts and historical aspects.

Japan is a smaller geography located between the giants like China and USA. It has waged war with both in past, got defeat from China and was nuked by USA. It is an ally of USA today, but it has a conflict of interests and geo-strategic security standoffs with the North Korea and China. It has continuously tried to reassert itself in the Asia particularly in the Asia-Pacific. These geographical peculiarities combined with the historical context of the Second World War if seen in the perspective of the contemporary economic development in association with the cultural ethos of Zain Buddhism, Japan has potential to adopt a new kind of foreign policy matrix in steadily multipolarizing world.

Sweden among the European nations has a classical history of cultural neutralism based on its geopolitical location near the gateway of Eurasia. It has vociferously refused to be part of international war alliances and has at least tried to exhibit neutrality, although it has been compelled at various times to withdraw its policy of neutrality. In the recent context of Crimean and Ukrainian conflict, Sweden was at the verge of weaponization due to security concerns.

Australian history is similar to the past of USA but has extremely different geo-political realities. It is situated in the one corner of the word; encircled with the largest rim of islands; and has always been amid geo-political issues related to maritime security. Over last one decade, like Japan, Australia has also tried to attain maximum space in Asia pacific. The trio of Australia, Japan and Sweden has played a considerable role in the international development through AUSAID, JAICA, and Sida.

Middle Powers and Culture of Old Guards: Australia and Japan have been trying to develop themselves as middle powers, in which they have been successful. They are the part of G20. They have got unexpected pace of economic development. Although Australia is a power of

Australian continent, it is considered in broader perspective an Asiatic economy. Sweden is a sizeable economy but have significant role in the world politics due to its policy of neutralism. There are possibilities that these countries tomorrow may develop as middle power and may ally with the countries like India, South Africa and Brazil. A similar position in the west is held by Germany, which is already a recognized world power.

There is also criticism by many corners over the roles of these three countries concerning their non-vocalism for the under-developed and developing nations as well as countries. There are also issues in some parts of the world that when these countries serve their economic interests in Asia-Pacific, South Asia, Middle East and Africa, they do not care much about the interests of indigenous people in the employment, royalties and Corporate Social Responsibilities (CSR). Besides, the attitude of these countries in wider terms is replica of the G5+1 regarding the overall legitimate secessionist movements in the world. These three countries are highly non-sensitive to the legitimate freedom movements like the freedom movement of Kurdistan in Iraq and Sindh and Balochistan in Pakistan. This rigidity among their policy framework is an outcome of their replicating the already recognized world powers. Besides, being a mediatory force they prefer to help support the developing counties and their statuesque despite becoming the supporters of change within their obsolete state-structures.

Growing Others: New powers are growing in almost every continent of the world. Germany, India, Brazil and South Africa are towards the path of middle power. What matters more that how these powers become reformative in bid to change the course of world politics statuesque since the global politics is changing very steadily. Canada may also play a similar role. And, the club could also have been joined by the powerful others like Israel and Iran who due to certain reasons are not part of it. For example Israel was and is potential enough to play a significant role. Had Israel and Iran not drained their energies in the decades' long conflicts, they would have been promising countries in the overall global development.

All of them, if engaged with the traditional as well existing world powers like USA, UK, Russia, France and China for the course changing politics, global economy transformation, reforms in the trade regimes like World Trade Organization (WTO) and fiscal oligarchies like World Bank (WB), International Monitory Fund (IMF), and Asian Development Bank (ADB), as well as further reformation in the bodies on Climate Change and Nuclear Nonproliferation the results may become highly friendly towards world citizenry.

Challenges Ahead

The biggest challenge of our times is a paradigm shift in the interest-games around the globe. There can be hundreds of ways to serve the interests in a manner to avoid damaging the legitimate interests of the indigenous people in the regions of high stakes. The other major challenge is to cleanse the dirt and straight the knotty patches that were created due to World War I, II and the Cold War.

Twenty first century has to get rid of the dirt and the trouble created in the twentieth century. We have to fight with the climate threats, poverty, food insecurity and non-sovereignty, struggle for the civil and political liberties in almost all continents of the world. The time has come for the world to transform quantitative voters' democracies of Asia and Africa into the substantive democracies. We have to give liberations to the nations like Sindhi, Baloch and Kurds that have lost their legitimate sovereignty two centuries ago and fighting for the freedom. In fact Sindh and Balochistan are the historical countries that are under subjugation since last 170 years.

Let the changing world power matrix also address the legitimate issues that have devastated nations and subjugated nations in Pakistan, and war victims in Afghanistan and Iraq. The most important would be putting a final and permanent full stop to the use of religious extremism as a proxy of the war to resources and geo-strategic interests. A large range of structural and legal framework reforms within United Nations in the above context is the niche of the time.

A real mid-path

An appropriately blending the philosophy of Gandhi, Tolstoy, Martin King Luther, Nelson Mandela and G.M. Syyed with the international relations and politics is the only way forward for peacefully co-existing world. Utopia or material? Only time has to prove.

Published in Daily Afghanistan Times on December 30, 2014

MAKING OF TWENTY FIRST CENTURY STATE

Wars are the history (or 'his-story' in terms of feminism) of our generations. The notion of a peaceful, harmonious, war-free, non-racists, non-extremists and non-chauvinistic world however has to find an appropriate path for the materialization not through the slogans but essentially through the real, practical and pragmatic transformations and reforms within and around the human society, and essentially within the state apparatus of the countries.

Juxtaposing to the theoretical aspects of anarchism, the time has not yet come for human society to cede from the institution of the state, because it will ultimately happen through the evolutionary process of transformation in and around the human society and the societal institutions. Therefore, a new world would be impossible without certain sets of reforms within existing state-apparatus in the various human societies. This ultimately would change and re-determine the nature and health of society-state relation and interaction.

Unmaking of wars

Wars, in the form of feuds, historically were the business of collective communities in the pre-class formation of society. Later on, this role was undertaken by the warlords of the fiefdoms and tribes. Due to industrialization and urbanization of human society on the broader scale, wars became a fundamental characteristic of the early nation-states. Today, war-making is no doubt a sole realm of the state authorities. The decisions of war-making today are taken in accordance with the proclaimed national, regional, continental and international interests.

In the political course of contemporary socio-economic history, a twofold set of stakeholders has emerged around the world that have a decisive say in the war-making process - the inter-dependence of weapon and natural resources industry, and narrowly limited states owned think tank groups.

The contours of this twofold phenomenon are basically the practices of a non-representative process of determining and defining the national interests, and the *unsustainable strategies* to attain these interests. An unsustainable strategy is a prolonged international engagement in a region or country which does not have appropriate exist strategy; has lesser or no human damages; minimum or no specific impacts on the ecology; and the indigenous population friendly framework. The broader loopholes in the strategic engagements, war-making around the world and unsustainable strategies for attaining interests have given birth today to a kind of global anarchy.

There can be two important aspects of possible global transformation in the context of state-society relations, and particularly with reference to the broader world peace. The world powers and the countries that have heavy-weapon industry may consider the investment and industrial infrastructure transformation to certain extent from weapon industries into soft defense technology so that at least niche of the trade and market demand factors behind the war-making may be minimized.

Since the developing countries are gradually becoming self-reliant in the basic heavy weapon industries, which is mostly owned by the states in the developing countries, the weapon industry into the developed world would ultimately shirk in upcoming decades due to natural reduction in the demand.

Besides, there is a highly important role of think-tanks in the statecraft, however one should not forget that without certain level of freedom as well as diversity of opinion and schools of thoughts, a think-tank institution or group would be unable to contribute appropriately to the state or the states. Thus, the degree of independence, if not neutrality, of these think-tanks is a prerequisite for the safer world.

In fact, a war-free world would only be possible if and when primarily the citizenry of the states and diversity of independent thinking process is also taken into consideration. This becomes a matter of high importance, when it comes to decide as well as define and redefining the national, regional, continental and global interests. Moreover, states should also consider redefining the state-private entrepreneur relationship.

Globalization disparity

The communication revolution and technological transformation has already started changing characteristics of the social classes. The globalization of the socio-political entities including class, technical and intellectual elite or the process of converting socio-political, technical and intellectual workers into the globalized elite is an outcome of the contemporary economic-relations and mode productions -- soft, hard, virtual and physical.

The current phase of industrialization and steady and voluminous process of urbanization in the world needs to be reflected and thought over through the deep analysis in a manner that a true and real phase of globalization based on the regional and continental parity almost everywhere be initiated.

Simultaneously, the globalization disparity among the various sections of a single human society, among the developed and rest of the societies and between the global north and the south needs to taken into analytical consideration so that a more appropriated and healthier process at the planning level may be kicked off.

Although this is bound to happen in the certain course of time since the technological and communication revolution would ultimately take human society towards that direction; however states, political groups, media and the social leadership of various nations need to foster the ingredients of the globalization-parity, vertically as well as horizontally, within and among the human societies.

Intellectual dilemma

There is a big difference between the degree and nature of freedom of thought before and after the Second World War. Human societies have no doubt successfully acquired the greater degree of freedom of thought both in terms of rights and collective responsibilities in the post world war scenario. However, the nature of freedoms has shirked, particularly after the mayhem of 9/11. This can be comprehended through the corporate and mainstream media, curbs on social media, state-defined matrix for the most of think-tanks and virtual control mechanisms to resist the freedom of thought.

Until nature of the freedom of thought is not redefined around the world, the transformation as well as reformations of the human societies as well as states institutions around the world would be impossible.

A new class

Over the period of last three decades, the class formation of human society is gradually acquiring the news layers - the social *virtuality*. It means that although the classical class composition, according to the Marxist interpretation does exist; the new aspects of the classes have emerged due to transformative shift in the mode of production and the technological revolution.

Thus, the new class characteristics can also be defined today as the 'virtual elite', 'virtual middle class' and 'virtual poor' for those whose position, influence and nature of work even contradict with their socio-economic realities of the class. It means a poor can also be considered elite if he is powerful in certain social realms more than rest of the poor or middle class person of his / her society or the contemporary poor or middle class person from the other parts of the world.

Creation of new states

The world today is victim of the overall trend of the global statuesque. This situation has caused ecology of international politics in which many a rotten and decades long world issues stands unresolved. The global as well as state level statuesque can be witnessed hitherto from non-resolution of the more than five decades old issues like freedom of Kurdistan, Tibetan autonomy, reconciliation between Tamil and Sinhala in Sri Lanka, and freedom of Sindh and Balochistan from Pakistan. These are the issues that have attracted lesser international consideration and media attention.

On the other hand, the issue of the futuristic transformation of Afghanistan is still not appropriately addressed. The recent handover of the training component of Afghan National Army to the Pakistan Army is one such example which essentially contradicts the principle of healthy transformation of Afghanistan because Pakistan has been the destabilizing and destructive factor for Afghanistan during the ISAF engagement in the war-fatigue land of Afghans.

This global as well as state level statuesque has deep roots in the non-representative determining of the national, continental and international interests. It also involves the issues like security at various level; globalization-disparity; the newly emerging virtual identities of 'powerful' and 'weaker' classes; and finally the nature of freedom of media and the individual liberty.

Reforms in the international community

United Nations (UN) not only needs to be reformed structurally, it also needs to undertake some essential reforms. A real United Nations would only be possible if and when it also forms a tier for the culture and civilizations in the broader fold of the UN in which various cultures that does not qualify the status of nation-states may also get an accredited membership in that United Nation's subordinate layer. This would encourage dying cultures; oppressed societies, social segments; ethno-linguistic groups; and representatives of faiths as well as ideologies to engage with the international community.

Besides, the procedures for the International Criminal Court and International Court of Justice needs further to be eased up at the level that crimes against humanity may easily to be taken to the international courts. Moreover, a forum for the federating state also needs to be created in the international body, where the intra-state issues may be addressed without any bloodshed or use of violence.

At the same time, a regional, continental and economic level permanent and non-permanent membership into the United Nations Security Council (UNSC) also needs to be introduced in accordance with the changing world. This will give an opportunity to offer the permanent seats in UNSC for emerging powers like Germany, India, Australia, South Africa and Brazil as well as permanent but non-veto seats of SAARC, ASEAN, Middle East, African Union, and Common Wealth of Independent States (CIS) of ex-Soviet states as well as Commonwealth of previous British colonies.

All these aspects of contemporarily required reforms are inter-dependent. Making a new world would be impossible without making a new state apparatus, and creating a free human society in twenty-first century, where all have their say within the international community forums.

Published in Daily Afghanistan Times and on the website www.merinews.com

THE NEW NEUTRAL

When individual or collective conflicts push politics into a blind alley, neutrality becomes key to mediation and resolution. Mediation, in all its forms—cultural, individual, collective or judicial—requires neutrality. If seen through the lens of diplomatic history among nations and the cultural history of people, neutrality embodied with justice has not only been successful in bringing about peace but also sustaining it. Hence, the diversified nature of conflicts, inter- as well as intra-state, ethnic and group require the exhibition of extreme neutrality for a judicious and sustainable resolution of the antagonism that is destined to lead all of us towards collective destruction.

No sides to take

Inter- and intra-state, ethnic and national conflicts have frequently occurred in the post-modern world. The post-World War League of Nations, which culminated into the UN, was an outcome of many international/European treaties among nations, which were neither judicious nor brokered by neutral mediators. Hence, it provided a reason for World War II. The two World Wars were waged between colonizers and aspirants holding colonial ambitions, seeking maximum control over colonies and their wealth and natural resources. Thus, the birth of the UN became inevitable since a neutral body was the niche of the modern era of statehood. Meanwhile, the powerful among the countries also formed parallel alliances at regional and international levels to further their interests.

No doubt, the UN has gradually transcended into a comparatively neutral forum since the world needed to go a step forward to formulate an international legal framework, not only for the member states but also for the citizens of member states. However, it is the our duty to introduce further reforms, agree upon new legal and policy frameworks, reform the structure and the authority to exhibit maximum neutrality and impartiality.

Nations, governments and international institutions always have to deal with a complex patchwork of relations and behaviors when they have to switch between neutrality and securing their interests. Since national interest has mostly superseded justice and neutrality in interest-based competitions, diplomacy and internal-external engagements, neutrality today has become an absurdity. This was evident in the recent political crises in Syria and Ukraine. It has also been observed in the Israel-Palestine conflict, the Kurdistan Movement, the Tibetan issue and the freedom movement in Sindh and Balochistan in Pakistan.

In fact, the absence of justice-based neutrality, both in nation-states and international and regional forums like the UN, Saarc and the Organisation of Islamic Countries, despite coming up with remedies have also been deepening the old wounds of the people. This has resulted in the rise of gross human rights violations, ethnic cleansing and war crimes that victimize millions of innocent citizens and dissenters.

Power biases

Power and interest-based politics and diplomacy have also given birth to another kind of discrimination. It is based on a discriminatory approach towards social leadership from the perspective of the oppressed or less powerful nations and ethnicities vis-à-vis monopolists and the powerful. The phenomenon is exclusively seen in broader civil society, which includes activists, journalists, writers, analysts, intellectuals, lawyers and other professionals. Usually, social leadership, associated with powerful ethnic groups, command more centrality and acceptability than leaders from among the group of oppressed people.

The phenomenon is more visible in the developing world, particularly in South Asian societies where social, institutional and structural development has historically been built around power. Pakistan, Bangladesh and Nepal are the best examples of this tilt. Since the Pakistani state and power corridors, for example, are monopolized by ethnic Punjabi allied with the Urdu-speaking elite, the rest of the South Asian and the world societies have an unintentional bias towards the social leadership of Sindhi, Balochi, Pashtun and Siraki origin vis-à-vis those of Punjabi and Urdu origin. This further intensifies issues of high importance and complex nature. The leadership of Punjabi and Urdu origin in Pakistan is well connected with the state, to which they have historically been given agency to participate in decision making. Their input is usually sought after by the establishment in almost all significant internal and external decision making. Besides, they also defend, in numerous cases, even unjustifiable decisions by the state in international forums in an overt or covert manner.

On the other hand, the leadership from Sindh, Balochistan, Khyber Pakhtunkhuwa and Siraiki Southern Punjab has been contributing intellectually to the social and political movements for rights. The journalists, human rights activists, scholars, intellectuals, academicians and literati from these provinces are not only discriminated within Pakistan but also during professional and thematic forums held regionally and internationally.

Similarly, when Baloch or Sindhi journalists, activists and thinkers are persecuted or killed by the state forces, the regional and international media and civil society seldom give them attention. However, when people of Punjabi and Urdu origin from the same professions—which are usually attached to certain layers of the establishment—are victimized, it becomes a matter of concern in regional and international forums.

If the Sindhi or Baloch leadership sympathizes with the political movement of their people and victims of persecution, the world outside criminalizes them. None would even think for the moment that the civil society and media associates and advisors of dominant ethnic groups in Pakistan have also an intellectual share in the crimes against humanity committed by the state. They are generally treated as credible entities. This inability to differentiate between social and civil leadership of the oppressed and the oppressor even by the leadership of other countries is also a kind of bias. Their unwillingness to see perceive both the parties as equals is also a kind of discrimination. It is an exhibition of the people-to-people or civil non-neutrality. This attitude is not only found among individuals but also those in highly reputable rights bodies, media houses, think tanks and intellectuals.

New ethos

A similar problem persists on a lower scale and in different forms when the leadership from the smaller countries, mostly with a single majority ethnic-construct like Nepal, Bangladesh, the Maldives and Bhutan engage and interact with their counterparts from the rest of the developing world. The non-existence of a neutral human interaction and people-to-people contact are more dangerous than that the foreign policies of the establishments of developing countries.

The critical mass of human rights, civil, political and economic justice and peace has grown in the last two decades. This larger tribe of activists, experts, journalists, writers, intellectuals, academicians and other professionals usually identifies itself with the various aspects and levels of social justice. Paradoxically, it lacks justice within its own tribe when it comes to supporting and sympathizing with victims or being neutral when it's a case of the oppressed versus the dominant. This not only applies to broader civil society but also international bodies. A new ethos need to replace old biases, discrimination and non-neutrality, primarily in people's diplomacy.

Published in Daily The Kathmandu Post on August 31, 2014

ABOUT THE AUTHOR

Zulfiqar Shah is a Sindhi stateless refugee analyst, journalist and activist currently staying in India. He is also author of 'Beyond Federalism: A socio-political history of Sindhi Nationalism in India (1843-1947) and Pakistan (1947-2012)'; 'Politics of Afghan Future' ; 'Decline of Pakistan' and 'Southasia Revisited'.